THE AMERICAN JOURNEY
THE SOMALI-AMERICAN
JOURNEY

by Rachel Castro

pogo

Ideas for Parents and Teachers

Pogo Books let children practice reading informational text while introducing them to nonfiction features such as headings, labels, sidebars, maps, and diagrams, as well as a table of contents, glossary, and index.

Carefully leveled text with a strong photo match offers early fluent readers the support they need to succeed.

Before Reading

- "Walk" through the book and point out the various nonfiction features. Ask the student what purpose each feature serves.
- Look at the glossary together. Read and discuss the words.

Read the Book

- Have the child read the book independently.
- Invite him or her to list questions that arise from reading.

After Reading

- Discuss the child's questions. Talk about how he or she might find answers to those questions.
- Prompt the child to think more. Ask: Do you know any Somali Americans? How are their cultural traditions similar to or different from yours?

Pogo Books are published by Jump!
5357 Penn Avenue South
Minneapolis, MN 55419
www.jumplibrary.com

Library of Congress Cataloging-in-Publication Data

Names: Castro, Rachel, author.
Title: The Somali-American journey / by Rachel Castro.
Description: Minneapolis, MN: Jump! Inc., [2020]
Series: The American journey
Includes bibliographical references and index.
Audience: Ages 7-10.
Identifiers: LCCN 2018058159 (print)
LCCN 2018059509 (ebook)
ISBN 9781641289238 (ebook)
ISBN 9781641289122 (hardcover : alk. paper)
ISBN 9781641289153 (pbk.)
Subjects: LCSH: Somali Americans–Juvenile literature.
Somalis–United States–Juvenile literature.
Refugees–United States–Juvenile literature.
Refugees–Somalia–Juvenile literature.
Somalia–Emigration and immigration–Juvenile literature.
Classification: LCC E184.S67 (ebook)
LCC E184.S67 C37 2020 (print) | DDC 305.893/54073–dc23
LC record available at https://lccn.loc.gov/2018058159

Editor: Susanne Bushman
Designer: Molly Ballanger
Advisor and Consultant: Abdullahi Aden, Somali Language Instructor, Minneapolis Community Technical College and Bilingual Program Assistant, Armatage Montessori School

Photo Credits: sadikgulec/iStock, cover (tl); Milosh Mkv/Shutterstock, cover (tr); Pixfiction/Shutterstock, cover (bl), cover (br); Michael Runkel/robertharding/SuperStock, 1; Anastasia_Panait/Shutterstock, 3; DE AGOSTINI/Getty, 4; Mark Pearson/Alamy, 5; mustafa6oz/iStock, 6-7; AFP/Stringer/Getty, 8-9; Phlippe Lissac/Getty, 10; hikrcn/Shutterstock, 11; Evgenia Parajanian/Shutterstock, 12-13; Helen H. Richardson/Getty, 14; Ahorica/Shutterstock, 15; Ken Hawkins/Alamy, 16-17; ROBYN BECK/Stringer/Getty, 18-19; Bloomberg/Getty, 20-21; MicroStockHub/iStock, 23.

Printed in the United States of America at Corporate Graphics in North Mankato, Minnesota.

TABLE OF CONTENTS

CHAPTER 1

LIFE IN SOMALIA

Mogadishu

Somalia is in East Africa. Most people here speak Somali. Mogadishu is the **capital**. It is on the Indian Ocean.

Somali **nomads** move a lot. Why? They look for fresh grass and water. They need it to raise **livestock**.

Most Somalis are Muslim. They practice Islam. Muslims pray five times a day. They have special **customs**. Like what? They wash their feet before they pray.

LEARN THE CULTURE!

Ramadan is an Islamic holiday. It is a holy month. Muslims spend time with family. They **fast**. At the end, they celebrate!

Somalia's ruler lost power in 1991. There was no government after. A **civil war** began. Many packed what they could and fled. Why? They wanted to escape war. They became **refugees**. As of 2019, there was still conflict here.

WHAT DO YOU THINK?

About one million people left their homes to flee war. They had to leave many things behind. They had to say goodbye to family and friends. How would this make you feel?

CHAPTER 2
COMING TO AMERICA

Many Somalis live in temporary homes. Many are in **refugee camps**.

refugee camp

Some of the camps are in Somalia. Others are in Kenya and Ethiopia. The camps are crowded. There isn't always enough food or clean water.

Some Somali refugees come to the United States. The U.S. government decides who comes to live here. They do **background checks**. These take up to two years! Most people do not pass the checks. The government helps those who pass. How? It gives small **loans** so people can travel here.

Welcome
United States
A Guide for New
Immigrants

PAS

TAKE A LOOK!

Look at this graph. It shows the number of Somali refugees who came here from 2008 to 2018. Which year had the most? Which year had the least?

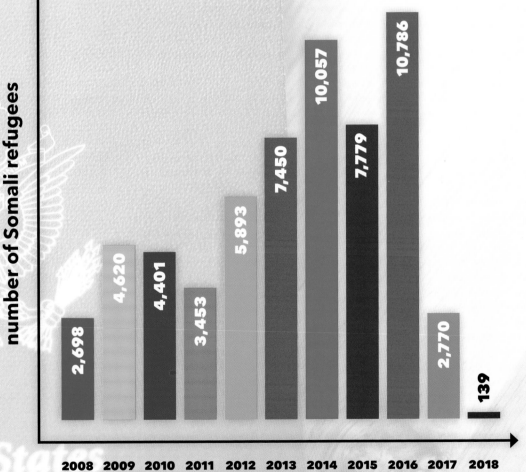

number of Somali refugees

2,698 | 4,620 | 4,401 | 3,453 | 5,893 | 7,450 | 10,057 | 7,779 | 10,786 | 2,770 | 139

2008 2009 2010 2011 2012 2013 2014 2015 2016 2017 2018

year

CHAPTER 3

A NEW HOME

Somali refugees experience new things. Like what? They learn English. They go to new schools. It can be hard. They can feel lonely.

They may feel cold weather for the first time! Minnesota has the largest Somali community in the United States. Why? Local groups welcome them. Some call this state their second home!

Minnesota

hijab

Americans learn about Somali **culture**. Some Somali females wear head scarves. They are called hijabs. Muslims celebrate holidays like Eid al-Fitr. It can be hard to find places to pray. They may face **prejudice**. They may face **stereotypes**, too.

LEARN THE CULTURE!

Meat preparation is special for Muslims. It needs to be blessed. It is sold at special stores. Some meat is not allowed. Pork is an example.

The path to citizenship is long. It is expensive, too. First, refugees must get **green cards**. Then they can apply to be **citizens**. They take English and history tests. The tests can be hard! People study.

DID YOU KNOW?

Somalia's president is Mohamed Abdullahi Farmajo. He is a dual citizen. This means he is a citizen of two countries. He is a U.S. citizen. He is a citizen of Somalia, too.

Learn About the United States

Quick Civics Lessons for the Naturalization Test

 U.S. Citizenship and Immigration Services

Ilhan Omar

Somali Americans make the United States their home. In 2018, Ilhan Omar made history. She was the first Somali American elected into **Congress**. She helps make laws.

Somali Americans are our friends. We live and learn together!

QUICK FACTS & TOOLS

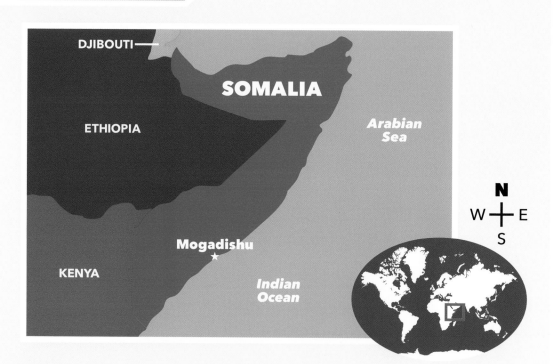

Number of Somalis who have left Somalia because of the civil war as of 2017: more than 1 million

Number of Somalis displaced within Somalia as of 2017: about 2.1 million

Number of Somalis needing assistance at the end of 2017: more than 6 million

Most common countries for relocation: Kenya, Ethiopia, Yemen, United States

Number of Somalis allowed into the United States in 2018: 139

Most common U.S. states for relocation: Minnesota, New York, Texas

GLOSSARY

background checks: Processes of collecting information to see what people have done in the past.

capital: A city where government leaders meet.

citizens: People who have full rights in a certain country, such as the right to work and the right to vote.

civil war: A war between people living in the same country.

Congress: People who make and pass laws for the United States.

culture: The ideas, customs, traditions, and ways of life of a group of people.

customs: Usual ways of doing things.

displaced: Out of one's home because of war, violence, or famine.

fast: To refrain from eating food or particular foods for a period of time.

green cards: Permits, called Lawful Permanent Resident Cards, that allow immigrants and refugees to live in the United States permanently.

livestock: Animals that are raised for food.

loans: Borrowed money that must be paid back.

nomads: People who wander from place to place.

prejudice: An opinion that is formed about a person or a group of people before getting to know them.

refugee camps: Temporary settlements that house people who had to leave their homes.

refugees: People who leave their home countries because of war, violence, or disaster.

stereotypes: Oversimplified opinions or unfair judgments about groups of people.

TO LEARN MORE

Finding more information is as easy as 1, 2, 3.

❶ Go to www.factsurfer.com

❷ Enter "Somali-Americanjourney" into the search box.

❸ Choose your cover to see a list of websites.

FACT SURFER